Manta ray

Spiney dogfish

Moray eel

Stingray

Whaler shark

Wobbegong

Whale shark

Nurse shark

Harbour Porpoise

White flanked porpoise

Bottlenose dolphin

Great white shark

Tiger Shark

Saddleback dolphin

Hatchet fish

Deep-sea squid

Bowhead whale *

Killer whale

Stomiatoid

Sperm whale *

Swallower

Deep-sea angler

*The animals with asterisks after their names are on the endangered species list.

DEDICATION

To Miranda, John, and Christopher

ACKNOWLEDGEMENT:

I wish to thank my colleagues who were so generous with their time and materials, particularly, Stanley Riel and Richard Cushman for authenticating the text and Mitch Schuldman for information on whale research. Thanks also to Evelyn Cronyn, my local librarian, whose assistance in tracking down materials was a great help to this country writer.

Library of Congress Cataloging in Publication Data

Miller, Susanne.
Whales and sharks and other creatures of the deep.

Summary: Introduces the physical characteristics and behavior of a number of sea creatures such as the spiny dogfish, orca, sea wasp, manatee, and coelacanth.

1. Marine fauna — Juvenile literature. 2. Fishes — Juvenile litera-ture. [1. Marine animals. 2. Fishes] I. Bonforte, Lisa, ill. II. Title.
QL122.2.M54   1982   591.92   82-8201
ISBN 0-671-45148-0   ISBN 0-671-46006-4 (lib. bdg.)

Whales and Sharks
and Other Creatures of the Deep

By Susanne Santoro Miller

Illustrated by Lisa Bonforte

Simon & Schuster Books For Young Readers
Published by Simon & Schuster, Inc., New York

Cradle of Life

Stegosaurus shook the earth with its every step about 190 million years ago. But as ancient as this creature seems to us today, it was a mere newcomer to the earth. The very first creatures on our planet were born in the waters more than three *billion* years before the age of dinosaurs.

Unlike the land dinosaurs, many ocean creatures have changed very little over the ages. The silvery-blue **coelacanth** (SEE-la-kanth) looks the same as its ancestors of 300 million years ago. The coelacanth's family, called lobe fins, was one of the most numerous fish in the ancient seas. Up until recently, scientists believed that lobe fins disappeared from the waters 60 million years ago. But, to their amazement, a live, snapping coelacanth turned up in a fishing net off the coast of South Africa in 1938.

The gentle **horseshoe crab** goes about its business today just as it did in prehistoric times. Like the coelacanth, it is the last of an ancient family line. Despite its hard shell, it's not a crab at all, but a distant relative of the spider. You may see it, by the light of the full moon, in May or June, crawling in with the tide to lay its eggs on the sandy shore.

Horseshoe crab

Coelacanth

Toothed bird

Ichthyosaur

Prehistoric whale

Clam

Starfish

Mussel

Near the Shore

The ocean and its creatures have interested us since the first humans gazed into a clear tidal pool. Let us begin a journey to the "cradle of life." We'll start close to shore, then move further out to the free swimming creatures. We'll see the huge, the small, the dangerous, and the strange. Finally, we'll travel to the bottom of the ocean to find out what's down there.

The first creatures that we'll meet may be familiar to you. If you've ever turned over a **starfish,** you've seen that it is built for life in the moving surf. Strong suckers on its arms hold it to rocks while the tide washes over it. These suckers can easily pry open a clam. Once the shell is open, the starfish simply pushes its stomach out through its mouth in the center of its star. Now it devours the clam right in its own shell.

Sea horse

Sea anemone

Hermit crab

The birth of young **sea horses** is one of the strangest on land or sea, because it is the father who has the babies! The female lays eggs in a pouch on the male's belly. Four weeks later, the father-to-be wraps his tail around a reed. Then he pushes his stomach in and out, sending about 600 tiny sea horses into the current.

The **hermit crab** is the housesitter of the sea shore. It never grows a shell of its own, but hunts for empty snail shells to make a home. That's not a plant growing on it, but a sea anemone. These flower-like animals attach themselves to rocks and shells along the shallow bottom. The graceful tentacles around its mouth open like petals but move like arms to catch and push in food.

Cephalopods

The octopus and squid belong to the family of cephalopods. Unlike many ocean animals, they have no tough skins or hard outer shells to protect them. Instead, they must use clever tricks to escape from their enemies.

Hiding is their favorite ruse. Cephalopods can squeeze their soft, elastic bodies into the tiniest underwater nooks and crannies. You might find them in narrow caves, old barrels, and even bottles. Of course, they can't spend their lives hiding. If caught out in the open, cephalopods shoot out a dark inky fog to cover up a fast escape. But most spectacular of all are their quick, dazzling changes in color. Like under-water magicians, cephalopods can take on the color of almost any background. Color reflects their mood, too. Pick up an octopus or squid and you will see a red, angry creature. Hold it a moment longer and you will see a white, frightened one.

The **squid** has ten arms: eight like the octopus plus two long tentacles with suckers at the ends. It's a powerful swimmer and moves its streamlined body by a kind of jet propulsion. It takes in water through openings in its neck, then forces it out and pushes backward. It can even shoot itself right out of the water!

Squid

Octopus

Clown fish

The **octopus** has eight arms, each with two rows of suckers. It has a bulky body and swims poorly. Timid and wary, it scoots along the sea bottom on its arms, hunting with sharp eyes for crabs and clams.

Jellyfish

Graceful, fragile-looking jellyfish drift with the ocean's currents in glowing colors like sunset clouds. Their bodies are very simple—just a stomach and a mouth. But they are not harmless. Three types of jellyfish are among the most deadly creatures in the sea.

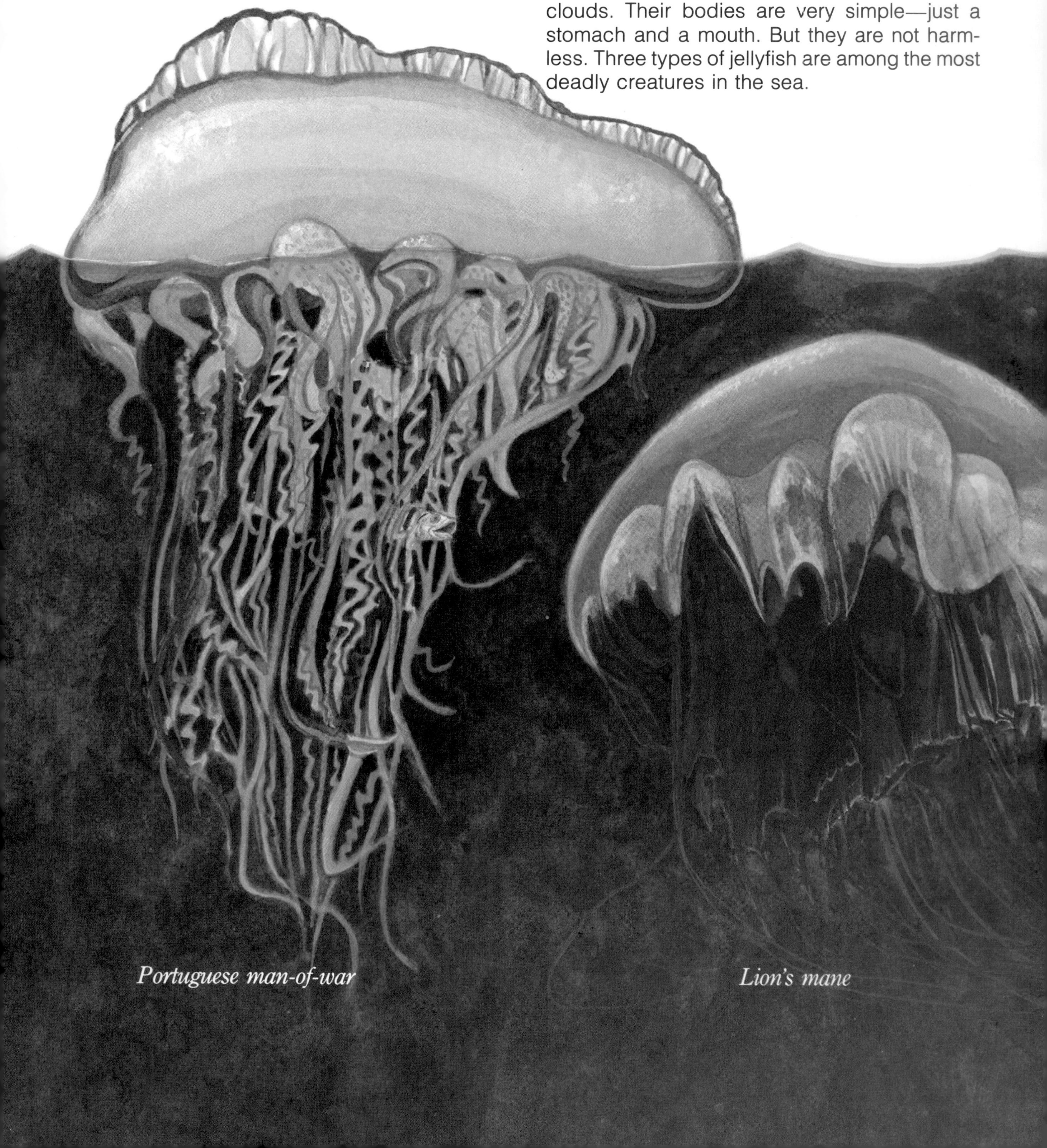

Portuguese man-of-war

Lion's mane

Like the battleship for which it was named, the **Portuguese man-of-war** rides the waves with plenty of weaponry. Its tentacles carry a poison that leaves a burning sting, and can cause cramps, breathing problems, and even death. Its body is filled with a gas that keeps it on the surface. Its tentacles stretch out beneath its body, as long as telephone poles.

In cold arctic waters, the **lion's mane** reaches an enormous size. Its body, called the bell or umbrella, is as big as an adult human. Its poisonous tentacles dangle as long as one hundred feet. It is so hardy that even after freezing solid, it can thaw out and spring back ready for action.

The **sea wasp** is the most dangerous of all the jellyfish—perhaps of all the ocean creatures. A sting from just one of its fifteen sticky tentacles can kill a human being in less than five minutes.

Common jellyfish

Sea wasp

Manatees

Can this be the original mermaid? It might not pass on close inspection, but the mother manatee, or sea cow, looks amazingly humanlike. To nurse its young calf, it raises its head and shoulders out of the water. Using its flippers as if they were arms, it cradles the young calf to its breast.

The manatee is a peaceful, fearless creature. It's content to live in shallow waters, grazing on the sea grass that would otherwise clog canals and waterways. It eats up to one hundred pounds of grass a day!

Like the whale, the manatee is a warm-blooded, air-breathing mammal. Millions of years ago, its land ancestors returned to the great spaces and food supplies of the ocean. Gradually, it adapted to life in the water, losing its hind legs and outer ears. A valve closes its nostrils so that it can eat and swallow under water. The manatee's closest land relative is the elephant. Can you see the similarity in their skins?

The manatee is like the whale in an unfortunate way. Both animals have had their numbers dangerously reduced by hunters. Their thick coats of fat, or blubber, are a source of oil. The manatee has also been hunted for its meat and leathery skin. Today, in the southern United States, it is often wounded or killed by motorboats that speed through once quiet waterways.

Further Out

Let us take leave of the shores now and move further out into the waters. Watch carefully, though, because the first two creatures we will meet can be quite unpleasant!

The **moray eel** is called the "rattlesnake of the deep." Like a snake, it likes to curl up in dark corners. If bothered, it will strike out. Its bite isn't poisonous, but it will leave a deep, jagged, and painful cut.

The moray's favorite meal is the octopus. It looks for the cephalopod in likely hiding places. When it finds an octopus, it doesn't stop to chew. It must eat quickly, because the moray breathes by taking in a constant flow of water through its mouth. Of course, if its victim is too big to swallow whole, it may just twist off and swallow one arm at a time.

Moray eel

In the Caribbean, the vicious **barracuda** is more feared than the shark. It has a slender, torpedo-shaped body, perfectly designed for speed and destruction. Its long front teeth are just right for grabbing and holding, while its small daggerlike side teeth slice its victims into bite-sized morsels. Those powerful jaws can easily snap a human leg in half!

The six-to-eight-foot barracuda prowls the daytime waters, often close to the surface, using its keen eyesight to look for bright, moving objects. It will attack an entire school of fish, slashing and ripping at its victims, then circling back to pick up the pieces.

Barracuda

Rays

One of the most incredible sights and sounds of the open sea is the great leap of the **manta ray.** Like an enormous bat, the manta spreads its wings twenty-five feet wide and soars up to fifteen feet over the water. Then, like a thunder clap, its 3,000 pounds crash back onto the waves.

Why does the manta leap? It's a great way to escape an enemy. It's also a dramatic way to scare off a trespasser. The jumps also shake off the fish's body lice. But the strangest leaps of all are those made by some rays just before giving birth. The pregnant female soars high over the waters, and its babies are actually born in the air!

The **stingray** spends most of its life on the ocean floor. It is very hard to see down there. Not only does its color blend with the bottom, but it uses its wings to fluff up a nice blanket of sediment before sleeping. Now it has only to doze until a likely meal swims by. Then it lashes out with its ratlike tail, leaving poisonous barbs to paralyze its victims.

Manta ray

Stingray

The Movement of a Stingray

Great White Shark

Sharks have always had a bad reputation. Even their name comes from the German word "shurke" for villain. It's true that most are unpredictable, and many are downright dangerous to humans. But some, like the great whale shark, are peaceful vegetarians.

Sharks are an ancient fish. They are so well suited for life in a variety of waters that they have changed very little over the last 300 million years.

The great white shark holds the record for the most attacks on humans. In 1919, for example, a great white went on a killing spree off the New Jersey coast. In ten days, four people lost their lives. The great white is fast and aggressive. Its jaws can crush a small boat. The average great white grows to eighteen feet and will weigh a ton and a half. But a few have reached thirty-six feet and tipped the scales at three tons.

The **wobbegong** is certainly a peculiar-looking shark. It is known by the name of carpet shark. Doesn't it look just like a lumpy, fringed area rug spread on the ocean floor? The wobbegong may remind you of a ray. In fact, the two fish are close relatives. Like the bottom-dwelling ray, it prefers the ambush method of hunting. It waits for a small fish to mistake its mouth flaps for weeds.

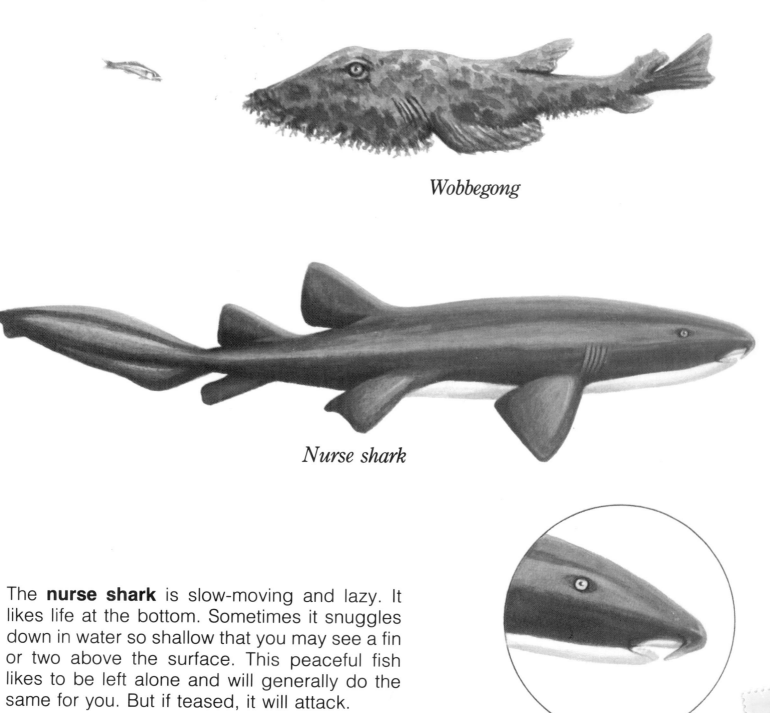

Wobbegong

Nurse shark

The **nurse shark** is slow-moving and lazy. It likes life at the bottom. Sometimes it snuggles down in water so shallow that you may see a fin or two above the surface. This peaceful fish likes to be left alone and will generally do the same for you. But if teased, it will attack.

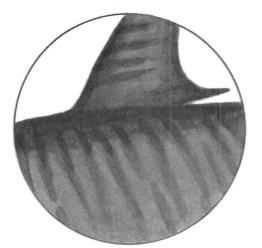

The **tiger shark** gets its name from its striped markings. It is a scavenger with a huge appetite. It eats just about anything—garbage at the bottom of bays, stingrays, turtles, other sharks, and humans. It's a clever hunter, too. Tiger sharks will swim slowly near the surface, then snatch up sea gulls as they touch down.

Tiger shark

Spiny dogfish

The **spiny dogfish** is one of the smallest sharks—usually only four feet long. Cod and herring are its favorite meals. Huge groups of a thousand slow-moving but hungry dogfish can mean bad news for fishermen. Although the dogfish is often no more than a nuisance, this little fish-eater is not entirely harmless. There's a poison gland in each of its spines.

Whale Shark

The whale shark is the largest fish in the ocean. When fully grown it is the length of a tractor-trailer truck. Like many huge animals, it is peaceful and confident. Divers can easily approach it. Some have even ridden it for short distances. It often lies perfectly still—apparently sleeping—right on the ocean surface. This habit—like napping in a driveway— has led to some unfortunate accidents with boats.

The whale shark feeds on tiny floating plants and animals called plankton. It cruises the seas with its six-foot mouth open, sucking in water, then straining it back out with its gill rakers, leaving plankton behind. Its 3,000 teeth aren't put to much use, but they are an impressive sight!

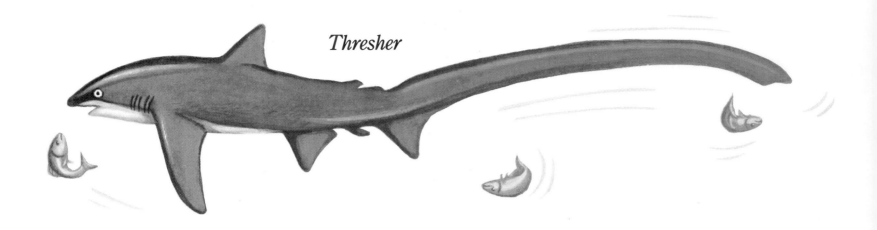

Thresher

Nearly half of the **thresher shark's** body is its tail. Can you guess how it is used? Here's a hint: a thresher is a farm machine that separates grain from the husk by beating or threshing it. Let us take a look at the thresher shark in action. A tasty school of fish swims into view. The thresher slowly circles around them, first widely, then in smaller and smaller circles. It whips at the confused fish with its huge tail, stunning some and driving the others closer together in panic. Finally, it has them where it wants them and attacks the helpless school, devouring them in quick gulps.

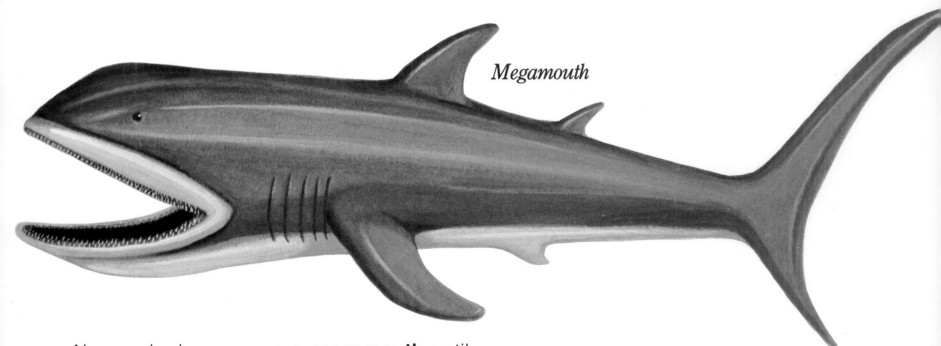

Megamouth

No one had ever seen a **megamouth** until November 1976 when it was hauled onto a US Navy ship, along with the sea anchor it tried to eat. The surprised crew had no idea what it could be. Megamouth was finally discovered to be a shark. You can see how it got its name. Its mouth is grotesquely wide, with thick lips and a top jaw that rises almost straight up. But strangest of all, that mouth glows in the dark! The light from this enormous cavern attracts deep-water shrimp and plankton, just like the neon sign on a diner that urges you to "EAT HERE!" So far, no other megamouth has been found. Doesn't it make you wonder what other unknown creatures are down there?

Hammerhead

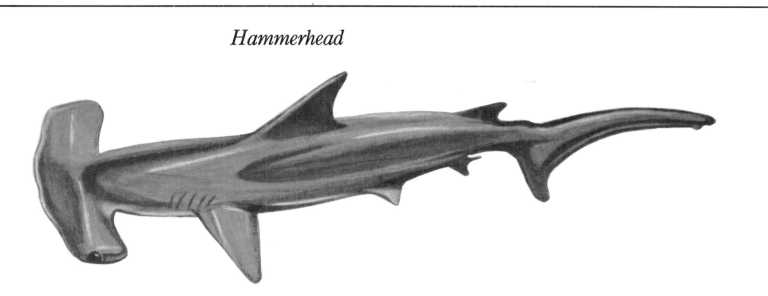

This is not a shark with ears or a fish with handles! Bizarre as it looks, the **hammerhead's** shape helps make it one of the sea's most keen and dangerous hunters. At each end of the "hammer" are an eye and a nostril. The far-apart spacing lets it see and smell over a very wide area. It locates its prey by balancing the scent between its nostrils. When the scent is equal in both, it knows the prey is straight ahead.

Whaler shark

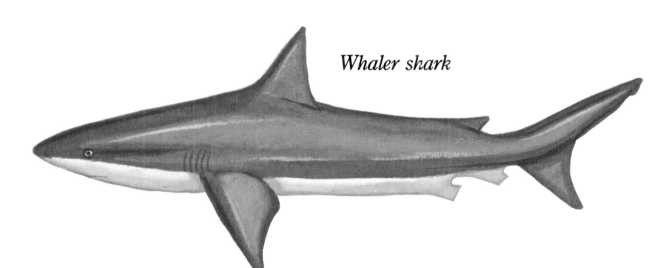

The whale hunters of yore gave the **whaler shark** its name. Schools of them swam about the ships, waiting for a whale to be harpooned. Then, when the dead whale had been fastened to the ship, the whaler sharks attacked the carcass, tearing off huge chunks. Today, these ten-foot-long meat-eaters prowl the Australian shores and are dangerous to humans.

Blue Whale

Whales are the great voyagers of the deep. At summer's end, when the polar sun is setting and the long winter night starts to close in, the whales begin their long journey to warm waters near the equator. There they will find mates and give birth. In the spring, they return to feed in the cold waters rich in krill, the tiny shrimp-like animals that are their main food.

Like the manatees, whales are warm-blooded mammals. They have lungs and must return to the surface to breathe air. Their spout is their breath, mixed with water near their blowholes. You can see the spouting best in the cold ocean air, just like your breath on a winter's day.

The gentle, intelligent whales have had a sad history. Since ancient times humans have hunted whales. This wasn't a problem until steam-powered harpoon boats began to speed through the seas, slaughtering whales in huge numbers. Today we can use man-made materials instead of whale products. Many, but not all, countries have stopped hunting whales.

The blue whale is the largest creature to ever live on our planet. It is twice the size of the biggest dinosaur. If that doesn't seem enormous enough, consider this: seven automobiles could line up on its back. It weighs as much as a small town of 2,000 people. It is the size of a schoolbus and weighs more than a full-grown elephant at birth. For the first six months of life, it grows two inches a *day* and gains ten pounds an *hour!*

Whales

Right whale

The **right whale** was the favorite prey of old-time harpooners. It was slow-moving and its blubber-rich body wouldn't sink after death. As a result of hunting, only about 1,000 right whales roam the waters today. Like most whales, the right whale is amazingly agile. It seems especially to enjoy *breeching*—lifting its forty-ton body almost completely out of the water.

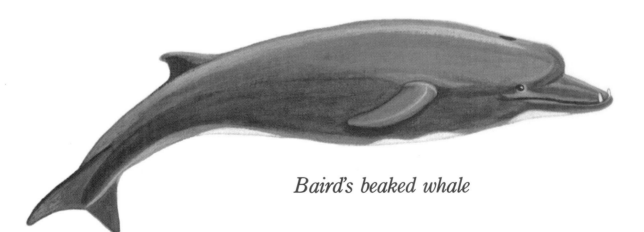

Baird's beaked whale

The **Baird's beaked whale** is a hard one to get to know. It's so alert, clever, and fast-moving that scientists have been able to do little research on it. We do know that it uses its two teeth to grab deep-sea squid. Those cephalopods are far beneath the waters, but that's no problem for the Baird's. It holds the record for dives—up to two hours! After a long dive, it stays on the surface for about ten minutes, panting like a long-distance runner. Then it's off with a graceful arc and a last flash of its tail.

Pilot whale

The little twenty-foot **pilot whale** travels in groups, or pods, of up to two hundred whales. They follow one leader, like autumn geese, and stay in tight formation. You can see the pod, not far from shore, keeping straight to their course, barely moving—not even for passing ships.

Bowhead whale

Like the bow of a ship, the **bowhead whale** raises its massive head above the cold waves. It is one of the few whales to spend the whole year in polar regions. The long fringes over its mouth are called *baleen* (bay-LEEN). Baleen strain its huge mouthful of water and trap thousands of krill. The bowhead's twelve-foot baleen, along with its extra-thick blubber, make it highly valuable to whale hunters. Just one bowhead could pay for an entire whaling voyage. The polar seas were once filled with 400,000 bowheads. Only a small pod of perhaps 600 remains today.

Humpback Whales

Streaks of light slant down through blue-green waters. A dark form slowly passes into view. Suddenly, an echoing cry breaks the underwater silence. The first long high notes are followed by deeper ones. Now a second voice joins in, then a faraway third, repeating the same notes. Over and over, for an hour or more, the sounds continue, like the slow warbles of a robin. This is the music of the humpback whales, and their strange, mysterious song fills the depths.

Researchers do not know what stories the humpbacks are telling each other. They do know that each year, all the whales in an area will sing the same song, and that each year will have its own six-verse song. It will begin like the last season's music, but change over the months.

Whales don't sing in the polar feeding areas. In those waters, where the whales just eat and sleep, the only underwater noises are heavy burbling sounds, very much like snores! They seem to save their music for the warm waters where they mate and have their young. Perhaps these are the whales' love songs, or maybe even their lullabies.

Whales

Gray whale

The Female **gray whale** is a gentle, protective mother. She raises her calves near the shore in sheltered bays. Unfortunately, this habit has also made her an easy target for whale hunters. The gray is also a favorite prey for orcas. Although it may be twice the orca's size, a gray will freeze with fear when hunted by one.

Orca

The **orca** is the only whale that feeds on other whales. Many, like the humpback or the gray, are even larger than itself. Orcas hunt in pods of twenty or more. They form a tight circle around their prey, they close in on them. Despite their savage behavior in the open seas, orcas are very intelligent and easily tamed. They steal the show in aquariums with leaps of up to twenty-five feet.

The **beluga**, or **white whale**, is a sociable and noisy creature. It likes to travel in pods of hundreds. Its calls and whistles to its fellow travelers have earned it the nickname "sea canary." Beluga calves are bluish-gray at birth. As they grow older, they lighten and change color. By the time they are six months old, they are a beautiful, pure white.

Beluga whale

Narwhal

Did you ever think you could find a unicorn at sea? The **narwhal** (Nar-wall) is the only known creature that has a single tusk. Its horn is actually a tooth that twists and grows—sometimes to nine feet. Scientists aren't sure just why the narwhal has a tusk. But since it spends much of its time in polar waters, it probably uses it to poke holes in the ice when winter fishing.

Sperm Whale and Giant Squid

Of all the terrible battles at sea, none can match the fury of the sperm whale and his ancient prey, the giant squid. The two are well matched. The adult squid, with a ten-foot body and tentacles stretching another thirty five feet, is as long as a three-story building. Only the enormous throat of a sixty-foot sperm whale could even attempt to swallow such a monster. In search of deep-water squid, the sperm whale will dive straight down over half a mile and stay there for up to ninty minutes.

Saddleback dolphin

Harbor porpoise

White flanked porpoise

Dolphins and Porpoises

Dolphins and porpoises are related to the whale family. As a group, they are intelligent, playful, and unafraid. Like whales, they find objects in the water by sonar. They send out clicking sounds which bounce off objects and echo, telling them where their targets are.

Bottlenose dolphins, shown here in a herd, are protective of each other. If one bottlenose is in trouble, it gives a "distress call." In just a few moments, all the nearby dolphins will rush to its aid.

Saddleback dolphins travel in groups of over a hundred. When they nap, they experience a watchful half-sleep, keeping first one eye closed, then the other.

The **harbor porpoise** is the smallest of the group. At only five feet, it's a bit longer than you.

The chubby little **white flanked porpoise** migrates, spending its summers in the Arctic and its winters in the seas from California to Japan. Tough pieces of gum stick out between its teeth to help hold on to wiggling squid.

Down Deep

Imagine yourself in a world that never sees sunlight. Imagine an ocean so deep and dark that no green plants can grow and the temperature drops to just a few degrees above freezing. In these nighttime waters, how could you tell a friend from an enemy? How would you find food or a mate?

Deep-water creatures have solved these problems in amazing ways. One solution is obvious. Just like campers in the woods at night, they carry their own flashlights! Many of the creatures you will meet in ocean waters 500 to 6,000 feet deep are *bioluminescent.* Their bodies actually produce light that attracts other fish like a lamp attracts moths.

As you can see, many of these creatures also have huge mouths. Food is scarce deep in the ocean, and once they get their mouths around a morsel, they want to make sure it doesn't slip away.

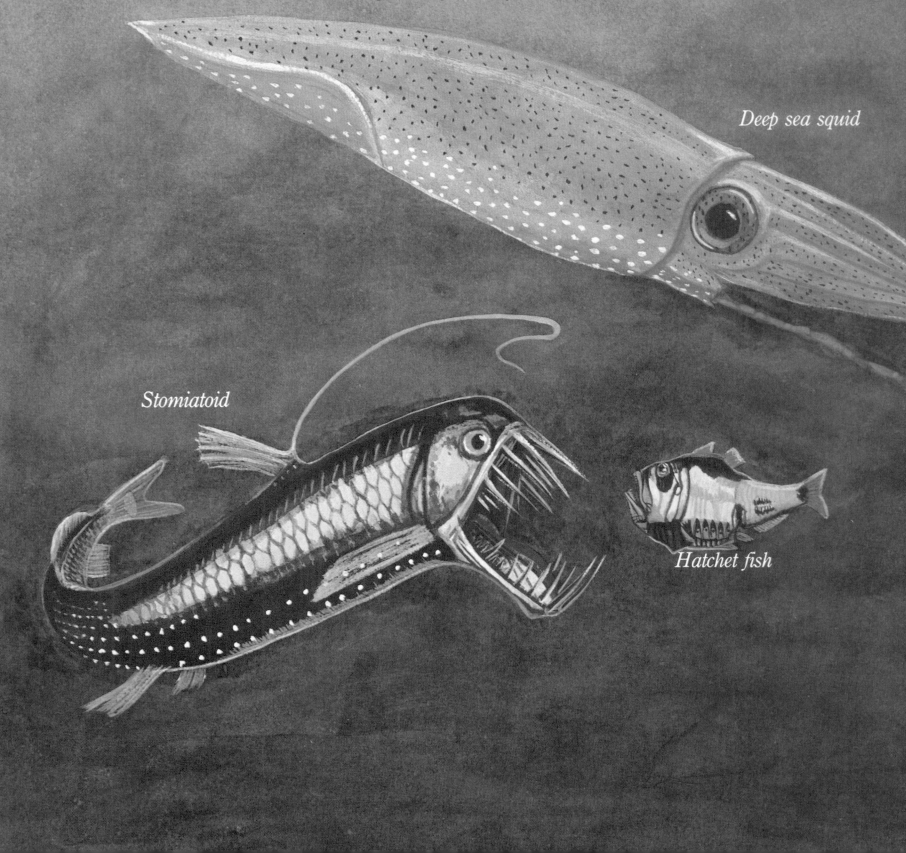

Deep sea squid

Stomiatoid

Hatchet fish

The **lantern fish**, no bigger than your finger, wears rows of glowing buttons on its head, belly, and tail. It spends its days in deep waters. At night it travels to the surface in large schools and flashes among the waves like a tiny lantern.

You can see how the **hatchet fish** got its name. Its tail spreads out like the handle and its body is as thin as the blade. It's just a tiny weapon, though, and would easily fit into the palm of your hand.

The **stomiatoid** (STO-me-ah-toyd) is also called the viper fish and the dragon fish. It grows up to a foot long and is just as vicious as it looks. In addition to the rows of lights on its underside, the stomiatoid attracts its prey with a long, glowing feeler. This feeler also acts as an antenna, telling the stomiatoid when a likely victim is near.

Like its relatives in more shallow waters, the **deep-sea squid** depends on an ink screen to make its getaway. But dark ink wouldn't be of much use in these midnight waters. Instead, it shoots out a glowing blue cloud. The sudden bright light blinds its enemy and off it scoots!

Shrimp

Angler

Lantern fish

Deeper

The six-inch-long **swallower** fish's jaw is hinged so it can drop open like a trap door. Beyond this deadly cave is a rubbery see-through stomach, allowing it to capture and swallow victims nearly twice its size!

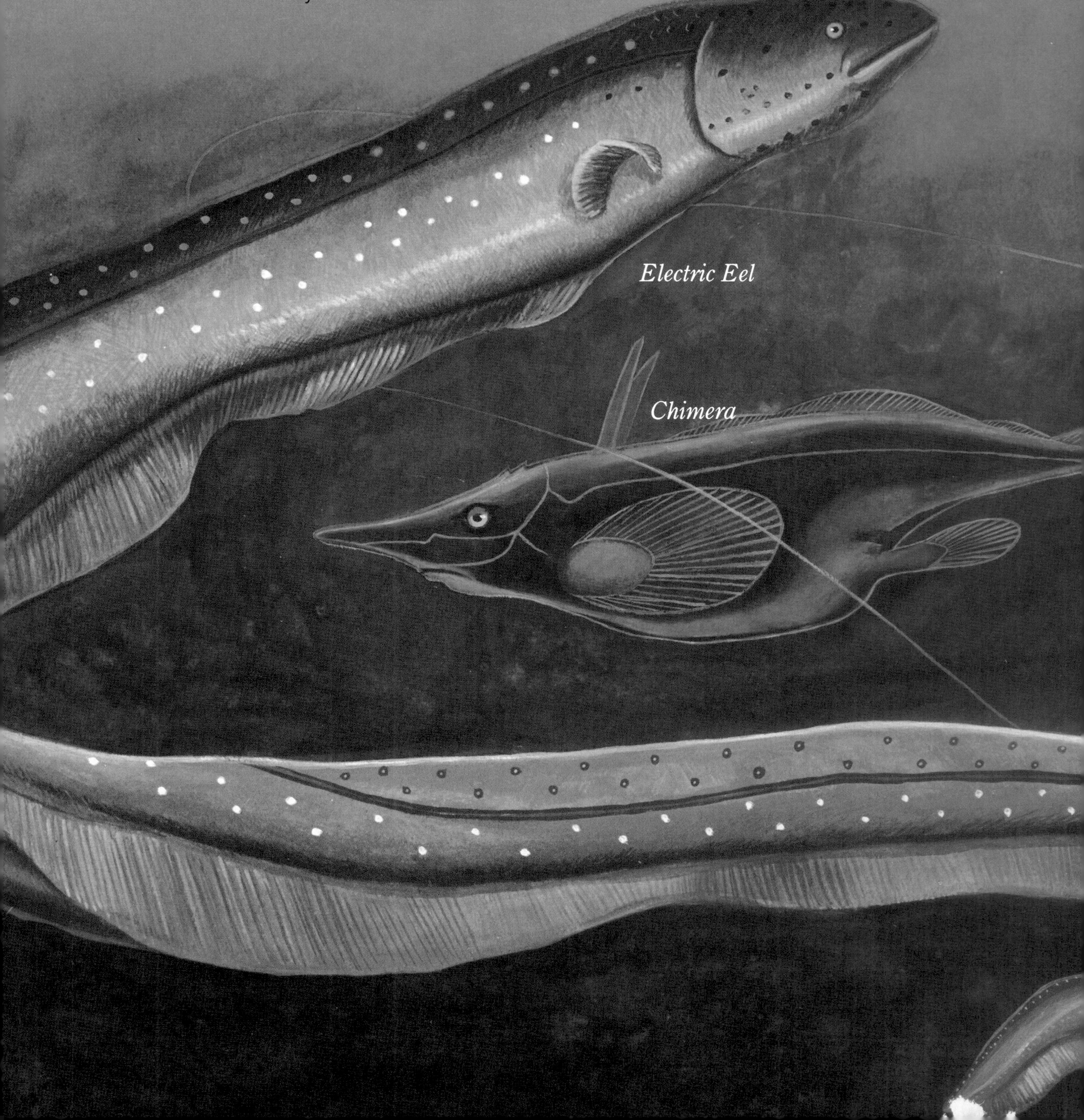

Electric Eel

Chimera

The original **chimera** (keye-MEE-ra) was a mythical monster with the head of a lion, the body of a goat, and a snake's tail. This deep-sea fish isn't quite that strange, but its appearance is certainly unusual. These ghost sharks, as they are known in some parts of the world, are members of an ancient family, whose line has changed little in hundreds of millions of years.

The **angler** fishes for its dinner a mile below the surface of the ocean. Patiently, the slow-moving creature dangles its glowing line, located around its mouth. When a curious fish moves in for a nibble, the angler's huge mouth drops open and sucks it in.

Angler

Swallower

Tripod

Deepest

Our underwater journey ends here in the very deepest part of the ocean. You see before you one of the great sea trenches. Like a V-shaped wedge, it slices into the earth more than six-and-one-half miles below the surface. Mount Everest, the highest mountain on land, would easily fit in here, and its top would still be more than a mile underwater.

The trench is cold, black, silent, and still. Many animals in this total darkness are blind and colorless. To help them survive the weight of all those miles of water above them, their bodies are soft and have no skeletons. Some spend their lives crawling slowly along the bottom, sucking up mud and feeding on bacteria. Others dig themselves right down into the ooze.

This remote outpost of ocean life holds a curious blend of the familiar and the strange. The sea anemone and the starfish here are very much like those we met near the shore at the beginning of our tour.

Deep-sea angler

Tripod

Pelican Eel

Beard worm

The deep waters are the last frontiers on our planet. Their mysteries were intact until recently. The *bathyscaph*, a diving vessel, gave us our first glimpse of the trenches. Scientists are now working on underwater robots that can collect samples and broadcast television pictures from nearly four miles down.

Will we ever know all the ocean's secrets? One thing is certain. Curiosity, and a sense of wonder, will lead us again and again back to the waters where life began.

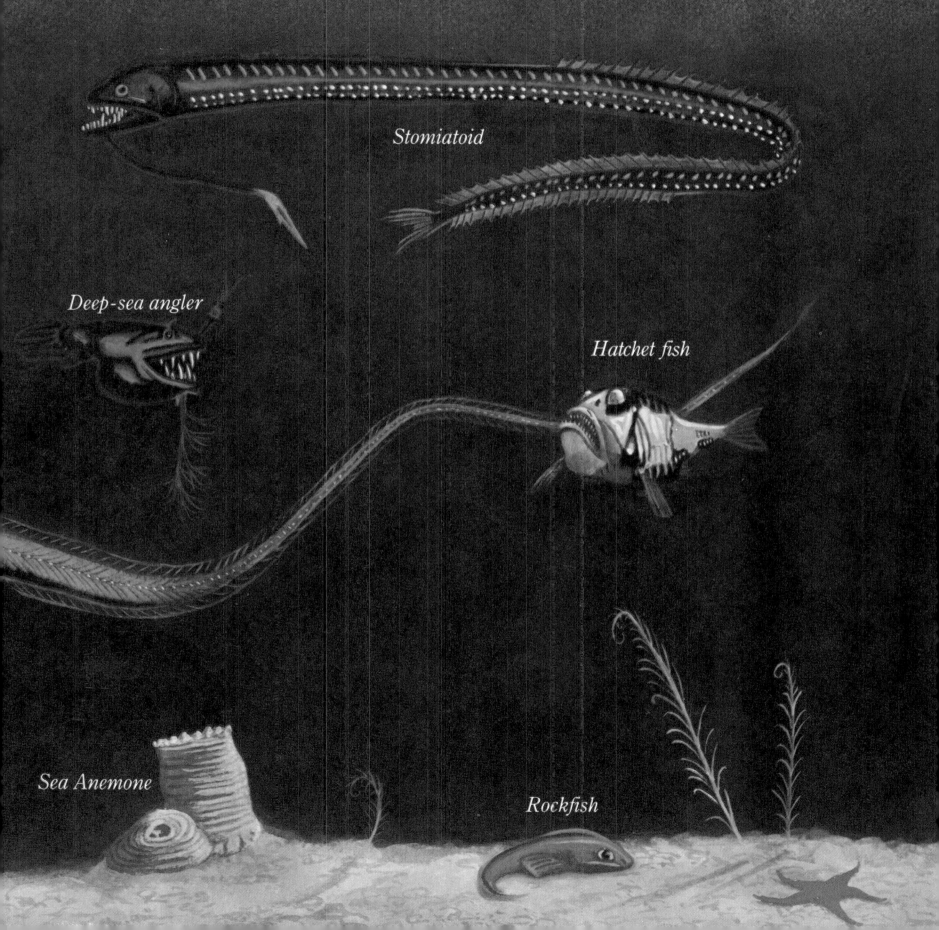

Stomiatoid

Deep-sea angler

Hatchet fish

Sea Anemone

Rockfish

1. *Narwhal*
2. *Beluga whale*
3. *Baird's beaked whale*
4. *Blue whale*
5. *Grey whale*
6. *Humpback whale*
7. *Megamouth*
8. *Octopus*
9. *Deep-sea angler*
10. *Bowhead whale*
11. *Saddleback dolphin*
12. *Pilot whale*
13. *Right whale*
14. *Killer whale*
15. *Lion's mane*
16. *Spiney dogfish*
17. *Stingray*
18. *Thresher shark*
19. *Horseshoe crab*
20. *Harbour porpoise*
21. *Tiger shark*
22. *Hermit crab*
23. *Sea anemone*
24. *Great white shark*
25. *Manta ray*

26. *Manatee*
27. *Barracuda*
28. *Nurse shark*
29. *Portuguese man-of-war*
30. *Hammerhead shark*
31. *Bottlenose dolphin*
32. *Giant squid*
33. *Sperm whale*
34. *Stomiatoid*
35. *Squid*
36. *Moray eel*
37. *Sea horse*
38. *Swallower*
39. *Whale shark*
40. *Coelacanth*
41. *Chimera*
42. *Common jellyfish*
43. *Starfish*
44. *Hatchet fish*
45. *Wobbegong*
46. *White flanked porpoise*
47. *Lantern fish*
48. *Sea wasp*
49. *Whaler shark*